P9-ELG-726

CHRISTIAN FAITH
THE BASICS

Walt Kallestad

Augsburg

MINNEAPOLIS

To my teammates at Community of Joy, where the basics of Christian faith are eagerly expressed and experienced continually.

A special thanks to:
- *Rose Jackson, who is a creative writing mate.*
- *Ron Klug, who helped me bring focus, clarity, and excellence to this writing project.*
- *Marv Roloff, who made the commitment to this project in bringing the dream to reality.*
- *New believers at Joy, who willingly shared their hopes, questions, struggles, and victories with me.*

CHRISTIAN FAITH: THE BASICS

Copyright © 1999 Augsburg Fortress. All rights reserved. Except for brief quotations in critical articles or reviews, no part of this book may be reproduced in any manner without prior written permission from the publisher. Write to: Permissions, Augsburg Fortress, Box 1209, Minneapolis, MN 55440.

Scripture passages are taken from the Holy Bible, New International Version, copyright © 1973, 1978, 1984 by International Bible Society. Used by permission of Zondervan Publishing House. All rights reserved.

Cover design by David Meyer. Book design by Michelle L. Norstad.

Library of Congress Cataloging-in-Publication Data
Kallestad, Walther P., 1948-
    Christian faith—the basics / by Walt Kallestad.
        p. cm.
    Includes bibliographical references.
    ISBN 0-8066-3397-2 (alk. paper)
    1. Theology, Doctrinal—Popular works. I. Title.
BT77.K24 1999
230—dc21   98-50128
                                                         CIP

The paper used in this publication meets the minimum requirements of American National Standard for Information Sciences—Permanence of Paper for Printed Library Materials, ANSI Z329.48-1984.   ∞ ™

Manufactured in the U.S.A.   AF 9-3397

03   02   2   3   4   5   6   7   8   9   10

Contents

Preface

ALL OF US STAND ON THE THRESHOLD OF A NEW MILLEN-
nium, a new thousand-year era in the history of the world
and humankind. Most of us, in North America and Europe
at least, live in a time of unprecedented technological gains
in communication, transportation, medicine, and scientific
discovery. We have a standard of living that the world has
not seen in the previous millennia.

But despite all the scientific and technological gains—
or maybe even because of them—many people experience
feelings of boredom, restlessness, emptiness, meaninglessness, and anxiety. There is a sense that something is missing—something essential for human happiness and fulfillment. And so people go on spiritual quests, looking for
something to give their lives meaning.

In their spiritual searching, many are looking again at
the centuries-old tradition of Christianity. If you are reading
this book, perhaps you too are examining the Christian
faith—either for the first time or looking again after having
been disconnected from Christianity.

Whether you've known God in your life for a long time,
you're seeking to know God more intimately, or you're just
curious to know what Christianity teaches, I want to encourage you to explore several questions with me: How can I know
God? Who is this Jesus? Why bother about sin? How do I
become a Christian? How do I live the Christian life? How do
I grow as a Christian? Is there hope for the future?

Truly exploring these questions means encountering God. Encounter changes us, whether it be an encounter with a person, an idea, or some aspect of the physical world. An encounter with the creator of the universe, who is actively and intimately involved in its day-to-day operation, has the power to change you profoundly and to enrich your life forever. I encourage you to be as open, honest, and objective in your inquiry, as I have tried to be in writing this book.

CHAPTER I

How Can I Know God?

A YOUNG WOMAN SAID TO ME, "THIS MAN LIVED IN THE SAME building with me, so I knew he existed. And on a particular Saturday, I could have walked through the door he held open for me and gone on my way. But if I had, I never would have come to know the man I've loved and called my husband for twenty-six years."

How many times has the pattern and quality of your life changed because you took time to stop and get to know someone? The same holds true for God. We can know *of* God, but that is not nearly the same as *knowing* God. How do you get to know God? Intellectually, I do believe there is a God. Experientially, I know God is real and I come to know God. We can begin to search for what God is really like, finding some answers to important questions of life in the process. Let's start with a basic question.

What proof do we have that God exists? How can I know there is a God if I can't see God? For thousands of years, atoms existed. Human beings didn't come close to imagining that atoms were the fabric of all physical matter—

including us. But did that mean atoms did not exist? It simply meant we didn't have the means available to perceive atoms. Now we can detect and even manipulate atoms. Scientists have pushed the boundaries inward to discover the existence of even smaller invisible particles with names such as quarks. How do we know they exist, if we can't see or smell, taste, hear, or touch them? Scientists detect them indirectly, by traces of their interaction with the world.

In a similar way, we can't perceive God directly with our senses, but we can perceive God indirectly. We can use our reason to think about God. We learn from the experience of others through the centuries (the Bible is a record of God's interaction with humanity). We can learn to identify God in our own life experiences.

The good news I want to share in this book is that God is knowable and wants to be known by us. God can profoundly and deeply enrich your life forever. Let's start with some basic thoughts about God.

GOD IS NOT A GOOD IDEA

For centuries, philosophers have found ways to think about God and have even attempted to prove God's existence, with arguments such as these: If there is a creation, then there must be a creator. If the universe seems to be designed, then there must be a designer. If there is a moral order throughout the world, there must be behind this a lawgiver. Arguments like these can help us come to a conception or an idea of God.

Christian faith says more than these arguments. Christian faith says that God is a person. Throughout the ages, men and women have spoken to and heard from God and have experienced God's power, presence, comfort, guidance, redirection, and other interactions with them. God is not just an abstraction. God is more than just a good idea. God is a being, and in some way each one of us reflects the image of God.

Saying that God is a person or a being does not mean that we have to think of God as an old man with a beard sitting on a throne somewhere beyond our solar system. Any time we think of God, we need to use picture-language or metaphors. But there are many other pictures of God in the Bible and human expense, such as creator, love, spirit, healer, rock, energy, mother, and many others. God has many names. Today, many people find it difficult to think of God as a certain gender. God, of course, is neither male nor female.

GOD IS CREATIVE

"In the beginning, God . . ." Those are the first words in the Bible, and they tell us an important truth: that we have not created God, but God has created us and the universe. God always makes the first move. God is a God of new beginnings, initiative, and creation.

Princeton biologist Edwin Carlson states: "The probability of life originating from accident is compatible to the probability of the unabridged dictionary resulting from an explosion in a printing factory."

One way we learn about God is by studying the creation. This means that science, done properly, can lead us to God. Christianity and science are not mutually exclusive. Science is a process of discovering how the things around us work. It focuses on the "know how" and not on the "know why." As a result, scientific discoveries lead to nuclear energy, cloning, and medical breakthroughs. But science cannot make value judgments or define morals or ethics. I believe science and Christianity, therefore, need to be complementary, not contradictory.

Understanding that absolutely everything comes from God helps us focus on what God has done, is doing, and will do for us. But it also tells us something very important about who God is. Why does God create? Because God loves us.

GOD IS LOVING

God is for us. God is always on our side, by our side, and even inside us. God is loving. The Bible goes even farther and says that God is love.

Too many people perceive God as a killjoy or an angry, judgmental tyrant, rather than as a tender lover. Certainly God does not overlook destructive actions and attitudes, but God's love steps in eagerly to reach out and help us, whether we are hurting or have done the hurting. Our best response is to let God love us.

My friend, Tom, said that when he went through the pain of divorce, he thought for sure the hand of God would strike him. Instead, he found God's hand reaching out to hold and help him. Tom said, "When I felt I deserved God's worst, God gave me God's best." God will never stop loving you, because God is love.

When we really take hold of these words—God is love—they become the most transforming words in the world. Discovering how much God loves you changes you so that you become more loving. When you are loving, you are helping make God's presence known in the world.

GOD IS COMPETENT

If God is big, then it is possible for me to live beyond my own limitations and liabilities. But if God is no bigger than I am, what I can achieve in my life is determined by my own human limitation. Christianity teaches that God is a God of unlimited power and unlimited resources. That taps my life into God's limitless possibilities.

God is bigger than our circumstances, competent to help with any need we have. Virginia was losing the battle against a rare autoimmune disorder. She lost weight and suffered headaches, jaundice, debilitating fatigue, and bleeding in her esophagus. Doctors told her that even a liver transplant might not be enough to reverse the disease. Surrounded by what seemed hopelessness Virginia chose to believe God was able to hear and help. She asked for her pastor and the elders of the church to anoint her with oil and pray for her. They did. And Virginia experienced a remarkable healing. "I don't use the word miracle lightly," she said. "Yet when I look back on my experience I find no other word that fits, no other concept that makes sense. God showed that he is bigger than any disease."

With the hand of a boundless God holding you hand and mine, we aren't limited by our own limitations. God is able!

GOD IS RELIABLE

Because God loves us with an unchanging and unlimited love, and because God is competent, we can rely on God. We can trust God. God keeps his promises. God has said, "I will never leave you nor forsake you" (Joshua 1:5). When we are tested, God can be trusted.

I met Audrey more than sixteen years ago. She and her family were new to Community Church of Joy. Within a few months, Audrey called me to say that her little girl, Michelle, was very sick. Not long after that, a decision had to be made to discontinue the life-support system that was keeping Michelle alive. Within a short time Audrey's mother died of a heart attack, her husband died in an accident, and her brother died of brain cancer. Audrey and her two daughters and the rest of us cried hard, but Audrey never once stopped trusting God to help her through it all. Her smile and words of hope continue to inspire everyone around her. She says, "The more difficult life becomes, the more I have discovered how reliable God really is."

Can God do anything? If God is loving and omnipotent, why doesn't he fix everything?

You and I are not preprogrammed computer chips. God created us with the ability to make choices. When we choose to abuse, cheat, or lie, the result is suffering and pain. God took a risk by giving us a free will, and our choices are not always what God would choose. When we choose badly, such as deciding to drive drunk, it isn't God's fault if an accident occurs. If we choose to spend more and more money on bigger houses or grander vacations or luxurious cars instead of giving money to feed the hungry, we can't blame God if people starve. Of course, not all suffering is caused by an abuse of our free will, but much lies within our power. We can ask God for guidance and wisdom in making the right choices.

How can God know and keep track of everything?

Neither time nor space limits God in any way. If we could explain the knowledge and understanding of God, he wouldn't be bigger than you or I. God *is* big. God is small enough, however, to live in human hearts. When God says that he knows when a sparrow falls or knows the number of hairs on my head, I can't explain it, but I can enjoy it.

How can I understand the Trinity?

As Christians have thought about and experienced God through the centuries, they have concluded that we can know God in three distinct but related ways.

God is our creator, our father, who made everything and who is above and beyond the world we know. God is the son whom we can know in human form as Jesus Christ (more about this in the next chapter). God is also the spirit, a presence that lives in the deepest part of ourselves.

Our limited human minds can never totally understand God. We have a very big God. We need the biggest picture we can get of God, and the teaching about the Trinity helps give us that.

Thoughts for Reflection

Through my scientific work, I have come to believe more and more strongly that the physical universe is put together with an ingenuity so astonishing that I cannot accept it merely as a brute fact.
— Paul Davies

God can be found. . . . There is a Divine Center into which your life can slip, a new and absolute orientation in God, a Center where you live with him and out of which you see all of life, through new and radiant vision, tinged with new sorrows and pangs, new joys, unspeakable and full of glory.
— Thomas Kelly

God wants us all, and he will not rest until he gets us all.
— A. W. Tozer

What were we made for? To know God. What aim should we set ourselves in life? To know God. What is the "eternal life" that Jesus gives? Knowledge of God. "This is life eternal, that they might know thee, the only true God, and Jesus Christ whom thou hast sent" (John 17:3). What is the best thing in life, bringing more joy, delight, and contentment than anything else? Knowledge of God.

—J. I. PACKER

An ordinary simple Christian kneels down to say his prayers. He is trying to get into touch with God. But if he is a Christian he knows that what is prompting him to pray is also God: God, so to speak, inside him. But he also knows that all his real knowledge of God comes through Christ, the man who was God—that Christ is standing beside him, helping him to pray, praying for him. You see what is happening. God is the thing to which he is praying—the goal he is trying to reach. God is also the thing inside him which is pushing him on—the motive power. God is also the road or bridge along which he is being pushed to that goal. So that the whole threefold life of the three-personal being is actually going on in that ordinary little bedroom where an ordinary man is saying his prayers.

—C. S. LEWIS

BIBLE STUDY

The Bible is one of our major sources for learning about God. You can dig deeper into the question of God by studying the passages below.

1. What do you learn about God from these biblical verses?

Acts 17:24-28   Jeremiah 32:17
Psalm 86: 5, 15   1 John 4: 7-12
Hebrews 11:6

2. "God is reliable" means that God keeps his promises. What does God promise in each of these Bible selections? How would your life be different if you believed each of these promises?

Jeremiah 29:11-13   2 Corinthians 9:8
Hebrews 13:5   Romans 8:38-39
2 Chronicles 7:14   Psalm 34:10

Questions for Discussion

1. What were your earliest pictures of God? What images of God help you most?

Father	Creator
Energy	Jesus
Spirit	Higher Power
The Force	Healer

2. Have you ever experienced the power or presence of God in your life?

3. What are the main questions you have about God?

4. Can you identify anything that stands in the way of your having faith in God? What might you do about them?

CHAPTER 2

Who Is This Jesus?

"I CAN BELIEVE IN A HIGHER POWER," AN EARNEST YOUNG woman said. "I am a spiritual person, but I don't see why I need to be concerned about Jesus. Honestly, is Jesus really all that important?"

More books have been written about Jesus than about any other person in history. Jesus still makes big news, showing up on the cover of *Time* and *Newsweek* magazines. Jesus is one of the most fascinating human beings who ever lived. But more than that, Christians believe that if you want to know what God is like, the best way to do this is to look at Jesus.

Although Jesus has been the subject of much controversy, there are some things we can know for sure. Let's start with those. Who is this Jesus?

THE MAN JESUS

We begin with our best source of knowledge about Jesus— the Bible, specifically the part we call the New Testament, and more specifically the four Gospels, written by Matthew, Mark, Luke, and John. These accounts of Jesus' life were written by eyewitnesses of Jesus or those with eyewitness sources. They were written during the first generation after Jesus' death.

The curtain goes up on the greatest drama in human history. Luke gives us a point of political business that pegs the event to a verifiable time and place: "In those days Caesar Augustus issued a decree that a census should be taken of the entire Roman world." This was the first census that took place while Quirinius was governor of Syria. Those days were the days of the Roman Empire, about 2,000 years ago.

Jesus' parents, Joseph and Mary, went to Bethlehem to be counted in the census. Because of the crowds in Bethlehem, Joseph and Mary had to stay in a stable. Some hay and a feeding trough was Jesus' first cradle. The first people who came to see the new baby did not include a Roman governor or religious leaders, but a group of poorly groomed shepherds.

Joseph and Mary took Jesus to live in Nazareth, a village in a remote area of Israel known as Galilee. Jesus grew up there, speaking Aramaic, the common language used in business. We know almost nothing of the details of Jesus' early life, but we can assume that he had a typical childhood. Because he grew up in a carpenter's house, he probably did household chores that included helping his father. Luke tells us that, as a twelve-year-old, Jesus enjoyed spirited conversations about religion with the spiritual teachers of his time.

As a young adult, perhaps about thirty, Jesus was baptized by a strange prophet who lived in the desert, a man we know as John the Baptist. After that, Jesus began the life of a wandering teacher, gathering a few disciples or followers who traveled with him to learn from his religious teachings. He was a master teacher and storyteller, often teaching in the form of stories known as parables.

Just about everyone agrees that Jesus was also a healer. He prayed for sick people and they got well. He touched blind people and they were able to see again. The deaf heard. The crippled walked. His compassion and love led him to reach out to all who needed him. People who came into contact with him had their lives changed.

Jesus enjoyed parties and went to dinner with just about anybody who asked him to join them. He was approachable and sensitive to people's needs, underlying thoughts, and emotions. People's credentials, or lack of them, meant nothing to Jesus. The shamed, despised, and outcast found forgiveness and worth when they met Jesus.

As we see him in the pages of the Bible, Jesus showed a full range of human emotions. He could be frustrated, angry, tired, and fearful; he was happy at a wedding party and wept when a friend died.

For about three years Jesus went about "doing good," as one of his contemporaries summarized. During this time many of the poor and a few of the wealthy heard Jesus and were impressed by his words and his actions. But Jesus also posed a threat to the establishment of his time—to the political and religious powers. They devised a plan to get rid of him. One of his own followers, Judas Iscariot, led a detachment of 'armed soldiers to capture Jesus at a park known as the Garden of Gethsemane, where Jesus had gone to pray. Jesus was taken into Jerusalem and there was beaten, mocked, and tortured.

Exhausted and already near death, Jesus was led out of the city to a hill named Golgotha and there crucified along with two criminals. Before his agonizing death, Jesus prayed for his enemies, saying, "Father, forgive them, for they know not what they are doing" (Luke 23:34). He also felt abandoned by God for a time, but moments before his death prayed, "Father, into your hands I commit my spirit" (Luke 23:46). Two followers of Jesus, at great risk to their own lives, removed the body of Jesus from the cross and placed it in a cave.

This could have been the end of the story, but in many ways it was just the beginning. On the third day after his death three courageous women went to the grave to embalm Jesus' body. They hurried back to tell the other followers that the body was gone. Soon, other followers of Jesus expressed the incredible news that Jesus was alive. God had raised him from the dead. For forty days, Jesus went among his followers. Hundreds saw him. And this good news transformed a ragtag, frightened assemblage of common people into an empowered, indomitable force that eventually changed the world.

Then Jesus left during the event we call Ascension Day. But he left his followers with two great promises: he would send them the Holy Spirit to live in them and empower them. And he was going to prepare a place for them where they could be with him forever.

Christians believe that if you want to know what God is like, you can look again and again at this man Jesus—at his words and his actions—and thereby come to know God.

GOD IN HUMAN FORM

But Christians went on to say this in another more striking way—that Jesus was God in human form. God became human to share our life fully, including all the weariness and frustration and suffering and even death. God did this to show us who God is. We can learn about God through various teachers and prophets, but to really show us who he is, God came to be with us.

You and I are important to God—important enough for God to come to earth and connect his character with his voice and touch. In the person of Jesus, God was on a mission to become more real and relevant to us. But more than that, God wanted to make the connection, to end for all time the separation between himself and us. God wanted access to our hearts, and Jesus was the way.

When I was twelve years old, I woke up in the middle of the night wondering, "Who is Jesus for me?" The question was so compelling that I went to my parents' bedroom and woke them. My dad got out a Bible and read to me, "For God so loved the world that he gave his one and only Son, that whoever believes in him shall not perish but have eternal life" (John 3:16).

After Dad read those words, I felt very warm and excited inside. I didn't have all the answers about who Jesus was, but I was convinced that he really loved me. My picture of Jesus today is still of one who loves me unconditionally. I believe that Jesus loves me so much that there is nothing I can do to change his mind. I can't imagine any greater news than to know that I am loved so much that the Son of God was willing to lose his life rather than lose me. When anyone discovers how much they are loved, nothing is ever the same. Life is worth living, no matter what happens.

In the person of Jesus, the creator of the world became human in order to develop an intimate relationship with human beings. And that included doing something about our sin, removing whatever separates us from God. We'll take a closer look at that in our next chapter.

Do I have to believe that Jesus did miracles in order to be a Christian?

No. What the Bible says is: Believe in the Lord Jesus Christ, and you will be saved. Looking to Jesus for salvation and being willing to follow him is enough to make you a Christian.

I can believe in Jesus as a great teacher, and even as a healer, but do I have to believe that he was God?

Yes. If Jesus wasn't who he claimed to be—God in human flesh—then Christianity is a hoax. What distinguishes Christianity from other religions is that Jesus is the promised savior of the world.

What is the most important thing for me to believe about Jesus?

That Jesus loves you. Period.

Why do Christians make so much of Jesus' death on the cross?

The Bible is clear that the penalty of sin is death. Because everyone has sinned, we are all under the penalty of death. However, Jesus Christ paid the penalty with his life for every sin ever committed. Death does not have the final word. God does. (More on this in chapter 3.)

How can we know that Jesus really rose from the dead?

Countless people testified that Jesus was alive. They actually saw his body and listened to his voice. Other evidence was that a well-guarded, sealed tomb was opened and empty. The most persuasive evidence is the faith millions around the world today have. I know Jesus is alive because he lives in me.

What difference does Jesus' resurrection make for us?

The difference Jesus' resurrection makes for us is the difference between life and death, hope and despair, joy and sorrow, heaven and hell, victory and defeat. The resurrection means that with Jesus anything is possible. Jesus promises, "Because I live, you also will live" (John 14:19). A fantastic future dawns for every believer, both today and forever.

THOUGHTS FOR REFLECTION

Christianity says that when God wanted to convey the truth about his infinite love for all [people], he made that love incarnate in a *single* life.
—KEITH MILLER

Then comes the real shock. Among these Jews there suddenly turns up a man who goes about talking as if he was God. He claims to forgive sins. He says he has always existed. . . . Now let us get this clear. Among Pantheists . . . anyone might say that he was a part of God, or one with God: there would be nothing very odd about it. But this man, since he was a Jew, could not mean that kind of God. God, in their language, meant the being outside the world who had made it and was infinitely different from anything else. And when you have grasped that, you will see that what this man said was, quite simply, the most shocking thing that have ever been uttered by human lips.
—C. S. LEWIS

To those who knew him, however, [Jesus] in no way suggests a milk-and-water person; they objected to him as a dangerous firebrand. True, he was tender to the unfortunate, patient with honest inquirers, and humble before heaven; but he insulted respectable clergymen by calling them hypocrites. . . . He was emphatically not a dull man in his human lifetime.

—DOROTHY SAYERS

Can you and I really have communion with Christ as we would with earthly friends? . . . I don't mean can we treasure his words or try to follow his example or imagine him. I mean is he really alive? Can we actually meet him, commune with him, ask his help for our everyday affairs? The Gospel writers say yes. A host of men and women down the ages say yes.

—PETER MARSHALL

Bible Study

Our most authoritative source about the life of Jesus is the Bible. Do some first-hand research in the primary sources to answer these questions.

1. What did Jesus teach about himself in these words?

    Luke 5:29-32   John 7:37-39

    John 8:12   John 14:2-3

2. To sample some of Jesus' teaching, read the following stories. What do you learn from each of them?

    Luke 10:25-37   Luke 15:1-7

    Luke 15:11-32

3. What do we learn about Jesus from these statements made by some of his earliest followers?

    Colossians 1:15-20   John 1:1,14

    Acts 2: 22-24

If you want to know more about Jesus, a great place to start is by reading one of the four Gospels in the New Testament. I suggest that you start by reading the Gospel of Mark. Contemporary translations, such as the *Contemporary English Version* or the paraphrase by Eugene Peterson called *The Message,* are the easiest to read.

QUESTIONS FOR DISCUSSION

1. What are your earliest memories of Jesus? What were you taught about Jesus as a child? What were your main sources of information about him?

2. If God came to us in the form of Jesus to help us to know him, then what can we learn about God from the life of Jesus?

3. If you could ask Jesus three questions, what would they be?

4. On the basis of what you now know and believe, how would you most honestly answer the question that Jesus asked some of his friends as they walked along a dusty road: "But what about you? Who do you say I am?" Remember that it is more important for you to give an honest answer, rather than try to give the "right" answer.

CHAPTER 3

Why Bother about Sin?

A FRIEND CALLED TO ASK ME FOR SOME HELP. "I DON'T do the things I want to do or things that I know are right. And the things I know are wrong and don't want to do, I do anyway. Where can I go to get help?"

My friend's question makes a good starting point for us to begin looking at an often misunderstood and basically unpopular word: *sin*. What is sin, anyway? What makes such an old-fashioned word such a contemporary problem? And does God have any solution for us?

THE REALITY OF SIN

Sin is not, as some people suppose, just doing bad things. Sin is what leads people to commit murder, steal, cheat on their spouses, abuse others, molest, pollute, engage in bigotry, and carry out acts of injustice and destruction. In our everyday language we call these kinds of acts sins, but in fact, they are symptoms of sin in our lives. So are bitterness, hopelessness, indifference, hatred, and other hurtful attitudes. Sin is a human condition that separates us from God, and this condition reveals itself in those negative, destructive acts and attitudes.

Still, it's hard for most of us to grasp what separation from God really means. Think of shopping with a toddler. Why do you see so many toddlers connected to a parent by a child harness or wrist strap? It's because a child's natural inclination is to resist what the parent wants, and to do what he wants, in his own way, in his own time and direction, with no clear understanding of the consequences. A loving parent realizes that this natural bent endangers a child's safety.

Sin is something like a self-willed child. It is our natural bent to want our will in our own way, on our terms, in our own time and direction—rather than naturally wanting to heed God's purposes, priorities, and plans.

Like a toddler, we often don't recognize the dangerous consequences we risk when we run through life apart from God. As Robert L. Short puts it in *The Parables of Peanuts:*

> All of us "originate" or come into life lacking the one thing we really do need, as it finally turns out—faith in our creator. This originally none of us has. None of us shows up in the world with God built-in or even with a built-in devotion to God, but only with a built-in devotion to the world itself.

Anyone who believes we naturally enter the world with a selfless love for others and the desire to do good hasn't spent much time on any preschool playground.

Our natural condition of sinfulness produces everything from a critical sarcastic tongue to genocide. The size of the act to attitude is not important. You can't be "sort of" sinful, any more than a woman can be "sort of" pregnant. The truth is that sin is sin, no matter how big or small, no matter how it manifests itself in our lives. It cuts us off from God's will, God's standards, God's timing, and God's love. Sin is the opposite of what God intended for our lives. Its consequences are emptiness, callousness, grief, anxiety, a hardened heart, a twisted perception of ourselves and the world, alienation—an almost endless list of ills and evils.

I have met people who say, "I don't think there is anything such as sin. There is no such thing as right or wrong." But when I start talking with them, I find out that if someone cheats them or steals from them or mugs them, they are quick to see it as wrong. Or when they look at conditions in the world such as violence in our cities, terrorist attacks, or acts of rape or murder, they believe these are very wrong.

Some people picture sin as taking a wrong path or an arrow missing the intended target or falling short of a goal. "Well, what's so bad about a slight misjudgment in direction or coming up short?" you may wonder. Nothing, if you're talking about a walk in the park or failing to match your best time in a 10K race. But what if your goal is to stop an epidemic of cholera?

What does it matter if we incorrectly pursue, miss, or fall short of goals? When the potential of the life God intended for each of us, connected intimately with God is not achieved, then falling short matters enormously. When our connection, our direction, our target, and our goal affects our life, here and eternally, sin endangers our existence.

You may be wondering, Well, why didn't God simply create us to be loving, trusting, and obedient? The reason is that God loves us. The great part about being a human being is that God gave us free will. But free will is problematic. On the one hand, it is good that we can make our own choices. On the other hand, choice creates a dilemma. And if we choose against God, it matters a great deal.

GOD'S SOLUTION FOR SIN

God took a huge risk in allowing us to choose or not choose to live in a relationship with God. When you love someone unconditionally, though, is there another choice? God saw that we would not always choose to be loving, to think pure thoughts, to have pure motives, to be free of jealousy, envy, or deceit, and to always trust him. God's solution for this dilemma was not compromise or permissiveness. Because God's powerful love for us could not allow him to lower the standards, God's solution was to make up the difference himself between how we live and how he intended us to live.

God provided, if you will, a "transformer" for our lives so that we can always be close to God if we choose. God did it by coming to us himself, embodied in the sinless Jesus.

How did his coming solve the problem of our failure to live perfectly up to God's standards? The Bible explains: "God made him who had no sin to be sin for us, so that we might become the righteousness of God" (2 Corinthians 5:21). This is what has been called the Great Exchange—Jesus' goodness is exchanged for our sin.

Jesus' death on the cross paid for our sins forever, put our hands back into the hands of God. Jesus is the transformer who makes it possible for each of us to live in connection with God. When we accept God's act of forgiveness through Jesus, God sees us as perfect, and the relationship between us and God is restored.

This was so important that God wouldn't leave the task of paying for our sins to anyone else. My friend and associate, Tim Wright, relates a story about a woman who had stopped at a truck stop to put gas in her car:

> As she pulled onto the freeway she noticed a truck pulled out and followed her. No matter how fast she went, the trucker stayed behind her. This went on for several miles until, absolutely panicked, she pulled off to the side of the road and jumped out of her car. As she ran away, she looked back and watched as the truck driver jumped out of the cab of his truck, ran to her car, threw open the back door and dragged

a man out of the back seat. To her horror, the woman realized that a would-be attacker had hidden in her car. The trucker had seen him and was trying to catch up to her to save her life.

That woman's experience isn't much different from the experiences that many of us have. We hear Jesus saying that we need a savior, but to be honest, we're not really sure why that is. We're not sure why Jesus feels we need saving. And that's because we're not necessarily aware of what Jesus came to save us from. But here's the answer: Jesus came to save us from death—the living death that is living sinfully, apart from God in this world, and eternal death that is separation from God after we leave this world. Like the trucker in the story, God foresaw the danger of sin in our lives, which we can't always see.

Saving is serious business. The price of paying for our sins was enormous. Jesus paid the price by sacrificing his life on the cross for us. Strong nails didn't hold Jesus to the cross; strong love did. The solution to the problem of sin was and is, forgiveness through Jesus' death. God's great driving desire for us to live in friendship and relationship with him led him to die on a cross to conquer everything that could ever separate us from him and destroy us. It led him to rise again to give us life abundant and eternal.

God himself paid the penalty for our sins because he profoundly loves us. God came in the person of Jesus and did for us what we could never do for ourselves—pay the penalty for sin. He gave us what we could never get for ourselves—eternal life. It cost God to love us that much. That is grace. That is what grace is all about. And grace is what Christianity is all about. God gave himself in Jesus, not because he was forced to, but because he delights in us. We have the great privilege to receive, enjoy, and celebrate this gift.

God's basic purpose for our lives is that we live in a love relationship with him. Rather than leaving us on our own to find the right path, rather than being exclusive and leaving people out, God made a way that invites and includes everyone. He became that path for us in the person of Jesus. The path that he offers is clearly marked and open to everyone, and it's guaranteed to get us home.

Great moral teachers and philosophers offer us wisdom about life. Only Jesus offers us life itself, through himself. As "the Life," Jesus ensures we'll experience all that life has to offer by removing those things that rob us of life: untruth, guilt, shame, hopelessness, and despair. In other words, the path to God is not about ideals, philosophies, or religion. It's about a personal relationship with Jesus, who leads us straight to the heart of God because he is God. Of all the religions in history, Christianity alone is not about what we do for God, but what God has done for us.

I encourage you today, if you're searching for truth and meaning, to follow Jesus. He is the way; he is the truth and the life. He is the answer to the deepest longings of your soul. He has come so that you don't have to walk alone anymore. He will walk with you and lead you home to significance and ultimate meaning.

Of course, I've done a few things wrong. But does God have the right to expect me to be perfect?

Yes. God does have the right to expect you to be perfect. God knows that anything less than perfection causes problems. If financial statements don't balance, a business can fail. If a husband is not faithful, a relationship may end.

God will not lower the standard, but God will make up the difference. That's costly, but that's what I really like about God.

Why couldn't God just forgive us? Why did Jesus have to die?

God can do anything he wants to do. Nevertheless God chose to send his only son Jesus Christ to pay the ultimate price to save us. Just as the penalty for a crime must be paid if there is to be justice, so the penalty for sin, which was death, must be paid. Jesus paid the price. Now all is forgiven.

I believe that Jesus died on the cross for me, but I still feel guilt. What can I do?

If you have honestly confessed your sins to God, your guilt is gone. You then need to let go of any lingering feelings of guilt. Holding on to guilt destroys the joy of being forgiven and freed. The moment any feeling of guilt pops up, pray: "God, this guilt is not coming from you. Please take it all away. Thank you."

THOUGHTS FOR REFLECTION

A dead soul has no life. Cut off from God, the soul withers and dies. The consequence of sin is not a bad day or a bad mood but a dead soul. The sign of a dead soul is clear: poisoned lips and cursing mouths, feet that lead to violence and eyes that don't see God. . . . The finished work of sin is to kill the soul.

—MAX LUCADO

We are told that Christ was killed for us, that his death has washed out our sins, and that by dying he disabled death itself. That is the formula. That is Christianity. That is what has to be believed. Any theories we build up as to how Christ's death did all this are, in my view, quite secondary: mere plans or diagrams to be left alone if they do not help us, and even if they do help us, not to be confused with the thing itself.

—C. S. LEWIS

Jesus did not die to save us from punishment. He was called Jesus because he should save his people from their sins.

—GEORGE MACDONALD

We may try other ways than God's ways, but they won't work. It won't do to say "everybody does it, so I'm no worse than others." You can't commit adultery and get any genuine comfort in knowing others who do. You can't cheat on a contract or on your income tax and find consolation in knowing that others cheat too. Nor can you lose your temper and speak cruel words to someone you love and brush it aside with, "Well, that's the way I am." You have generated memories that will clamor for some place to rest. They will roam your soul like ghosts until you put them in the only place that can divest them of their power—before the cross of Christ.

    —ALVIN N. ROGNESS

BIBLE STUDY

1. What do you learn about sin from these Bible passages?

    Romans 3:23   Romans 6:23

    1 John 1:8   Romans 5:12

2. What do you learn about God's remedy for sin in these words from the Bible?

    John 3:16   Romans 5:6-8

    1 John 4:10   2 Corinthians 5:21

    Ephesians 2:8-9

If you want to explore the subject of sin and salvation further, read Romans 5.

Questions for Discussion

1. What were you taught about sin? How do you now understand the word *sin?*

2. Do you think many people today are concerned about guilt? What do people feel guilty about? What do you think is the answer to guilt?

3. What do you think God expects from us? What does God desire for us?

CHAPTER 4

How Do I Become a Christian?

MY SON PATRICK AND I DECIDED TO CHECK OUT THE availability of Phoenix Suns basketball tickets. Because every one of their games was sold out, our chance of getting tickets was remote. To our amazement, the ticket office found two $18 tickets in the "nosebleed section," as high up and far away as you could get and still be in the building.

After a steep climb we found our seats, caught our breath, and settled in. Only moments later, two other fans appeared and informed us that we were sitting in their seats. Though we had legitimate tickets, an usher informed us that we would have to give up our seats to the newcomers. He took us to a security desk and, with a twinkle in his eyes, said, "Merry Christmas!" Looking down at the tickets he held out to us, we saw that the price was $72 each. When we found our seats, we realized that they were two of the best seats in the arena, right behind the Suns' bench.

What a gift! A gift we had done nothing to earn. And that's what Christian faith is about. God saw humanity's situation as sinners, came to us personally in Jesus, and gave us the best gift we could possibly have, better than we could imagine, and without our deserving it.

Now when the usher held out those $72 tickets, all Patrick and I had to do was to accept them. It's a simple truth sometimes overlooked: someone may give me a gift, but it is not truly mine unless I accept it. We could have refused them, but then we would have missed out entirely on the excitement of the game.

THE GIFT OF GOD

God came to us in Jesus Christ and did for us what we could never do for ourselves. God gave us what we could never get for ourselves. Christianity is about God's power and performance, not ours. Our relationship with God does not depend on our being religious or earning our salvation by going to church, reading the Bible, praying, or helping others. The radical truth is that Christianity depends on how good God is, not how good we are. When we realize God gives his gift freely out of love, we free our hands to receive it. We simply need to accept.

All I have to do to enter a right relationship with God—all I can do—is trust God's gift of salvation through Jesus. Trusting God is simply the practical application of faith. Intimacy with God comes through knowing Jesus, and that begins with trusting him to be exactly who he claimed to be.

Accepting Jesus is agreeing with God that you are sinful and need the forgiveness that Jesus' death and resurrection provide. Accepting is acknowledging that you are forgiven through Jesus. This focused faith produces trust in God and obedience toward God. That's what it means to be a Christian.

What God calls us to do is that simple. Furthermore it is a "person-to-person" call. No one can receive this gift for you. You cannot inherit salvation because your father, mother, grandparent, or any relative was or is a Christian. Salvation is not inherited by human blood, but merited by the blood Jesus shed on the cross.

It's significantly simple. Take time right now to answer these questions. Do you believe that Jesus is who he said he is, the son of God? Do you believe you are sinful and need forgiveness? Do you believe that Jesus died on the cross and rose from the dead to forgive you and to give you a new relationship with God? Do you want to live your life God's way?

If you answered yes to these questions, you have accepted God's gift of salvation. You are a Christian and you have eternal life with Jesus.

WHO NEEDS THE CHURCH?

When you accept God's gift and become a follower of Jesus, you do so as an individual, but you immediately become part of a great family, the Holy Christian Church, which includes all Christian believers, regardless of their denomination. This Holy Christian Church is not some big organization. It is what the Bible calls "the body of Christ." It is the means whereby each person can carry out the life of Jesus in teaching, healing, and loving. God loves the church and wants the church to be healthy, life-giving, and faith-building. The church is important to God and to God's people.

You will also want to be a member of a local church. You need the church because it's too hard to be a Christian alone. No, actually, it's impossible. It's like being an ember totally detached from the fire. No isolated individual can receive or contribute to helping the fire burn brightly.

How can you get the most out of your membership in a church?

1. Find the right church for you.
Finding the right church is one of your most important decisions. Finding the right church for you may not be easy. In most places, fortunately, you have plenty to choose from.

I should tell you right away that finding a perfect church is impossible. But finding a church that meets your needs is possible—I mean your needs for solid biblical teaching, for a place to worship God, for supportive fellowship, for a place of prayer, for opportunities for service. Look for a church that will meet your needs and those of your family, if you have one. Creative churches are radiant life-giving places. Healthy churches are open to new methods and styles without compromising truth and solid thinking. It may take you a while to find the right church, but the search is worth it.

One of today's dangerous attitudes is: "What have you done for me lately?" If you shop from church to church only to see what you can get, you miss the greatest rewards of membership: giving your time, your talents, and your treasures.

2. Commit to it.

Without commitment, nothing significant will happen to you or through you. Knowing how important commitment is, it is essential that you find out what you are committing to. Most effective churches have a sharply focused vision and mission statement that you can read and consider before you make a commitment. Once you discover what is important and commit to the vision and mission of the church, you are in for one of life's great adventures. Great churches are churches where people have made great commitments.

3. Participate in it.

The more we commit to involvement, the more satisfied we become and the more rewarding our church experiences are. As an athlete, I've sat on the bench as well as played in the game. I can assure you it's a whole lot more fun participating than sitting. Participation is the key. Getting the most out of our church comes from participating through serving rather than watching.

What form should your service take? Fortunately the church offers many ways to participate. You'll probably be happiest serving where your gifts match the needs of your church and community. That could be in singing, teaching, maintenance, community service, working with children, visiting older members of the community, working in the political arena, or countless other areas of life.

4. Support it.

The truth is that God owns everything. What we have is simply a gift. There is a test every person takes in life. It's called the money test. This test is evaluated by how much we keep for ourselves and how much we give away.

The bottom line is that nobody can ever give more than God. If everyone who went to church gave 10 percent of their incomes to God, I am convinced that all the people in the world would have food to eat, clothes to wear, medicine to share, people to care, books to read, seeds to sow, clean water to drink, and a church in which to worship God. One person can't do it all, but together we can. It starts with people like you and me.

5. Promote it.

As the senior minister of Community Church of Joy for twenty years, I have watched the church grow from a few hundred to the many thousands who participate today. This growth happened because friends started bringing their friends to church. More than 90 percent of the people who ever come to any church do so because a friend invited them.

The main thing in life is to have a personal relationship with God through Jesus Christ. If that really

is the bottom line of life, then all of us need to pro-
mote it with our lips and with our lives. Imagine what
a fantastic community we would live in if everyone
were meaningfully connected with and participating
in church.

What about Baptism?

From the first days of Christianity, Christians joined
the church through baptism. Baptism signaled that a
person was beginning a new life, becoming a member
of a new family different from a human family. Today
Christians still become members of the church
through baptism.

There are some differences in the way Christians
celebrate baptism. Some churches baptize infants as
well as adults. Infant baptism is a sign of God's grace,
acknowledging that God makes the first move. It rec-
ognizes that our being in a relationship with God
depends on God's action rather than our intelligence
or our efforts. These baptized infants are seen as beginning a process of Christian growth that through the
work of the Holy Spirit will lead them to making a
personal commitment to Jesus and to God's way of
life. Other churches baptize only adults, stressing the
element of human response and commitment.

Either way, baptism signals that our sins are
washed away. Baptism marks the beginning of a daily
process of repentance, that every day our old selfish
nature is "drowned" and our new nature, the transformation that God wants, takes place moment by

moment. Living out of this identity as a baptized Christian, a member of God's family, each Christian goes on to live a life transformed by God's love. We'll look more at the shape of that life in our next chapter.

I still have many doubts about various aspects of the Christian faith. Can I be a Christian anyway?

Yes, you can be a Christian and still have doubts. Even the people who lived and walked with Jesus admitted their doubts. Doubts are part of our human condition. The key is to dare and doubt our doubts by giving them to God. Doubts diminish when faith is strengthened through worship and reading God's promises in the Bible.

How can I know which of the Christian denominations is right? It all seems confusing to me.

Denominations provide diversity and offer choices. They emerge from different perspectives and understandings of the Christian faith. Cultural distinctiveness also shapes denominational practices. Don't worry about the differences. Focus on the common threads that are tied together around God's promises, truths, and commands.

Why are some Christians mean and judgmental?

Some Christians have areas of their life they have never given up to God. These may include being judgmental, arrogant, critical, negative, or mean-spirited. Being a Christian doesn't make someone perfect. It means that one is loved and forgiven even though they still have faults and fail. I like the bumper sticker that reads, "PBPGINFWMY". It means, "Please be patient. God is not finished with me yet."

Church seems to be for the people who have it all together. How would I fit in?

Church is more like a health club than a saints club. When you go to a health club, you don't go because you're perfect in every way. You go to work out what needs to be changed, improved, or maintained. People don't go to church because they are prefect, but they go to get perfected. Perfect people don't need church, because they are already dead and in heaven!

My life is already so busy. How could I find time for church too?

All of us find time to do what we value most. We all crowd our life with things that are important to us. We use our busy schedules as excuses for not doing something. But getting involved in church has the highest time-reward value of anything anyone could possibly do because we are enriched mentally, emotionally, and physically.

THOUGHTS FOR REFLECTION

The Gospels recount how Jesus, having lived a perfect and blameless life, accepted a death of horrible suffering on the cross on our behalf, as an atonement for the sins we have committed. . . . Putting our faith in these concepts is what is meant by being "born again." It's when there is an intimate melding of my life with that of Jesus.

—JIMMY CARTER

One of your most important tasks is to find friends who want to walk with you on the long road of conversion.

—HENRI NOUWEN

We cannot be a community of one. To be a Christian is to be part of a community of friends that supports us in an ongoing life. This is what is known as a tradition; that is, something that transmits life. We need the support of an ongoing life-bearing community, the Body of Christ, the church.

—RACHEL HOSMER AND ALAN JONES

Baptism is not a ten-minute ceremony that happens to babies. It takes a lifetime to complete. Martin Luther called baptism "the daily garment which the Christian is to wear all the time." That is, the pattern of our Christian life comes from the continuous arc of baptism—begin brought low, washed, and then raised up. Every day is a new experience of that cycle: recognizing our sin, remembering that we are baptized as children of God, and then being invigorated by the assurance of forgiveness.

In baptism we discover that our relationship to God is not based on what we do, but what God in Christ has done. The ground of our relationship to God is mercy and forgiveness rather than justice. So each day we need to remind ourselves of God's mercy and forgiveness.

—H. George Anderson

If you're unhappy with your church, you'll find little comfort in shopping around for a church that will never fail you. And you'll find no comfort at all in giving up on all churches. You can hardly expect to keep your flame of faith glowing if you go it alone, drawing no warmth from others.

Churches do fail. For one reason or another, most congregations have an occasional bleak stretch. But unless the gospel itself has been lost, a dry period in the life of a church may set the stage for a fresh burst of the Spirit. It would be a pity to abandon the journey just as the road leads over the crest of the hill to new and exciting vistas.

—Alvin N. Rogness

Bible Study

1. What does each of these biblical passages tell you about how one becomes a Christian?

John 1:10-13   Romans 10:9-13
Ephesians 2:8-9   Philippians 1:6

2. Read Ephesians 4:1-16. What kind of life does the writer envision for the Christian community?

3. Read Colossians 3:12-17. What does Paul call Christians? List all the phrases that tell what Christians are expected to do.

4. What does each of these Bible passages teach you about baptism?

Matthew 28:18-20   Mark 16:16
Romans 6:1-4

QUESTIONS FOR DISCUSSION

1. How would you describe the spiritual life of the family in which you grew up?

2. What has your experience with the Christian church been so far in your life?

3. What would you like the church to be for you now?

4. Were you baptized as a child? If so, what has that meant to you? If not, what might baptism mean for your life in the future?

CHAPTER 5

How Do I Live a Christian Life?

THERE ARE SOME SERIOUS MISCONCEPTIONS ABOUT Christian life floating around in society. To see Christian life clearly, we need to examine some common attitudes.

DEBUNKING CHRISTIAN LIFE

If I become a Christian I will have no more problems.

This idea may seem ridiculous to you, but there are some eager Christians who believe that having Christian faith will erase all their problems. It's true that few of us like problems or struggle. But simply being a Christian won't eliminate them. Problems need to be solved.

On the other hand, we tell our children that nothing worthwhile in life comes easy. We'd be aghast if teachers told our children about math but never assigned them any problems. Deep down we know that a life of ease does nothing to build character, and yet this is what some people have been told to expect when they become Christians. They lose sight of the fact that succeeding in anything entails some difficulty or hardship, some trial or struggle that we must overcome.

Some people falsely believe that Christianity protects you from suffering. If that were true, Jesus would not have suffered. We have a Savior who suffered, and who still shares our suffering. He never promised us that we wouldn't suffer. In fact, Jesus told his first followers, "In the world you will face persecution. But take courage: I have conquered the world!" (John 16:33).

What Jesus promised to deliver was—and is— victory. Christianity doesn't promise the easiest life, but it does offer the best life. Jesus said, "I came that they may have life, and have it abundantly" (John 10:10). Jesus keeps that promise and gives us abundant life even in the middle of problems and pain.

Billy Graham knows that, and it helps him find strength to live a winsome life in spite of Parkinson's disease. In his book, *Just as I Am,* he said:

> Someone asked me recently if I didn't think God was unfair, allowing me to have Parkinson's and other medical problems when I have tried to serve him faithfully. I replied that I did not see it that way at all. Suffering is part of the human condition, and it comes to us all. The key is how we react to it, either turning away from God in anger and bitterness or growing closer to him in trust and confidence.

The Christian life doesn't mean living trouble free. It does mean confidently looking to God despite our circumstances, and relying on God's unfailing love, power, and guidance at work in us and in our lives.

If I become a Christian, I won't have any friends.
Becoming a Christian does not mean that you'll lose all your friends. Some cults require that, but not Christianity. God doesn't want us to isolate ourselves. Of course, you may find that, as you change and grow, you will form new relationships.

Christianity is about making healthy relationships—with God, with others, and with ourselves. God wants us to let go of unhealthy thoughts and actions. However, God also wants us to get involved in other people's lives in ways that will encourage them and show them God's love, truth, and forgiveness.

Living as a Christian doesn't just make you better at being a friend. It gives you something in common with people you may never previously imagined as friends. It opens up a whole new set of possibilities for solid, lasting friendships.

In addition to that, a Christian is never friendless because Jesus himself is our friend. A young woman said:

> When I was religious and trying very hard to be good, I was also very lonely. While I was flipping through radio stations trying to find my favorite country western music, I heard a pastor explaining how to invite Christ into my life. I did as he said, and my life started changing. I lost the fear and the feeling of being alone that had been tormenting my life. As I have gone through difficulties in my life, I have had the assurance that I am not alone and that all will be well. From Christ, I get the peace I need.

If I become a Christian, I won't have any fun.

Some people also mistakenly assume that becoming a Christian means throwing away fun. Maybe it's because they know some Christians who look like they've been "baptized in vinegar." But this impression may exist because what our society considers "fun" is sometimes of questionable value or even destructive. Some people think that going out on Saturday night and getting "hammered" is fun, until they face up to the consequences the next morning.

Whether it's drinking, drugs, gambling, or other "fun" pastimes that promise a constant high, when the thrill wears off, it takes more and more destructive living to recapture the thrill. God wants to rescue us from those kind of addictive and destructive games. The real truth is that God never asks us to abandon joy, cheerfulness, happiness, or a good laugh. Joy is the hallmark of authentic Christianity.

God doesn't offer us a relationship in order to drain all the joy and fun out of life—far from it. The things God tells us to do actually maximize our potential for lasting happiness—with no painful side effects. Because of Jesus and the forgiveness, new life, power, hope, comfort, and friendship he offers us, the Christian life can be a dance of celebration—even when times are difficult.

If I become a Christian, I will have to give up all my freedom.

Admittedly, there are "religious" people who try to

play God and assert do's and don'ts—primarily don'ts—for others to live by. I grew up being told it was wrong to dance, play rock music, wear lipstick, play cards, or even go bowling. Unfortunately, too many people find it easier to state what they think Christians are against rather than what they are for.

When Jesus was asked what the most important "rules" for life were, he answered, "Love the Lord God with all your heart and with all your soul and with all your strength" (Deuteronomy 6:5). This is the first and greatest commandment. And the second is like it: "Love your neighbor as yourself" (Matthew 19:19).

It's that simple. Jesus lived out the example of what God wants from us. Loving God and loving others as Jesus did is the gauge by which we're to measure our attitudes and actions—not rigid adherence to human rules or fashions.

Does that mean we Christians are free to do whatever we like? No, that would only be a form of slavery to our own desires, addictions, and compulsions. That would be a serious misuse of God's grace. Christian faith actually offers us more freedom, not less, because God's amazing grace makes us eager to do what God wants.

Through the Holy Spirit, God offers us the day-by-day power to break free of the habits, beliefs, actions, and attitudes that hold us in bondage. The Holy Spirit helps us grow more and more into the "me" that God intended each of us to be. That's real, radical freedom.

Living a Christian Life

We've now debunked some misunderstandings about the Christian life. It's time to look at the positive side. What makes Christianity a good way to live? As we've seen earlier in this chapter the Christian life offers us:

1. God's help and support in the midst of our problems and struggles.

2. A healthy relationship with God, with other people and with ourselves.

3. Genuine joy even in hard times.

4. Freedom from the things that enslave us and the power to become the best self that God intends for us.

In addition, Christianity gives us a model and image of what human life should be like. The best model is Jesus. As we saw in chapter 2, if we want to know what God is like, we can look at Jesus. But it is also true that if we want to know what it means to be truly human, to be the kind of person God wants us to be, we can do no better than to look to Jesus. Jesus is more than a teacher of good ideas or rules for living. He embodies that life, and now he puts his spirit into us so we can embody that life too.

Christianity offers us purpose for living. We are set free from meaninglessness and purposelessness, to discover our true reason for living. We do this as we cooperate with God, learn to discover our gifts, and come to use them for God's purposes in the world.

Some time ago, I was having breakfast with a very successful banker. A serious look came to his face and he said, "I have spent sixty-one years of my life making money. It hasn't been as fulfilling as I had hoped. With the rest of my life I want to make a difference. What shall I do?" This led to a meaningful conversation about the rewarding life of Christianity. I told him Christian life is about making a different world. Purposeful Christian living brings contentment of the heart and soul. Living all and only for Christ is what God intended when we were born.

We finished our time praying that every remaining day of his life would be dedicated to loving and serving Christ at home, at work, in the car, at parties, in the neighborhood, and on vacation. Today, I watch this man live a life beyond what he ever imagined. He is experiencing life as it was intended to be lived.

All this doesn't happen on the day you become a Christian. We all come into God's kingdom with all our bad habits and warped attitudes. God begins his transforming process in us. Sometimes he proceeds very fast and people experience remarkable changes. But becoming our own best self usually takes time. It's something we have to grow into. And that is the topic of the next chapter.

How can I know what God wants me to do with my life?

Simply ask God to show you. As you search your passions and gifts and dreams and talents and desires, you will discover what God wants you to do, be, and become. God's call is an invitation to participate in something significant that God is doing. It's not just a job, it's a calling. Jobs never satisfy; a calling does. Answering God's call leads to more than success; it leads to significance.

Why are so many Christians such bad examples of Christian living?

Some Christians have acknowledged that Jesus is their Savior, but they have not wholeheartedly surrendered themselves to Jesus as Lord. They trusted Jesus for their eternal life while still wanting to control their earthly life. That decision (or lack of decision) causes Christians to live far beneath their privileges and potential. The solution is complete and humble surrender, sacrifice, and service to God's way.

I'm a Christian but I still struggle with depression and addictions. Is there something wrong with my faith?

People not only still struggle after becoming Christians, but the way can actually get tougher. Christianity is not the easiest way to live, but it is the best way to live. Jesus has overcome sin, death, and the power of evil. Christians are on the winning team. Battles with depression and addictions can be severe, but God has many ways to help us. Ultimate victory is assured through Jesus Christ.

THOUGHTS FOR REFLECTION

There is no one way in which to live as a Christian—no standard pattern. And that's as it should be. Because you are not a human clone, a "type," or a "case." You are who you are. And, according to my understanding of this faith, it is the aim of the gospel to help you to become who you are, who you are *essentially;* not to impose upon you some completely new sort of personhood, but to give you the courage, imagination, and will that you need in order to grow into the really *human* person that is already there in you, potentially, waiting to be born.

—DOUGLAS JOHN HALL

What if we understood spirituality primarily in terms of *fidelity to the ordinary demands of daily living*—that is, persevering through whatever radiance or grayness each day may bring? Getting carried away by heavenly things because we've given up on earthly ones is not the call of God. The aim of the Christian journey is not to have ecstatic experiences of God (although this might occur), not personal fulfillment (although this might occur as well), but to share in Christ's incarnational ministry and mission in the world.

—ALAN H. SAGER

If you want to be happy and healthy, try being an "inverse paranoid." An inverse paranoid is someone who thinks everyone is out to make him happy. Try it. It works. Just imagine everyone you meet is trying to bring happiness and joy to your life. And then try to do the same for them.

—RICH BIMLER

The crisis of the human spirit in our time is the crisis of knowing what things are worth paying attention to. For a follower of Jesus, the discipline of spirituality is not so much of praying effectively as of paying attention effectively to the proper matters.

—MICHAEL WARREN

I can be truly happy when I have come to the place where:

• I feel accepted by God when I feel most unacceptable to myself. I recognize my need for God.

• I can really feel the empty places in my life. I can let others know when I am hurting and share the grief of others without embarrassment.

• I don't have to be the strong one all the time. I can be tender and gentle with people. I've given the control of my life to God and I don't have to "win" all the time.

• I want to know God and his will for my life more than anything. I am more excited about God's will for the world than my own financial gain, success in my career, or acceptance by my peers.

• I can enter into the feelings of someone who is hurting, lonely, or distressed. God has given me a sensitivity for the suffering of others.

• I can be completely open and honest with God and others—transparent. I don't have to pretend to be what I'm not.

• I really work at keeping the channels of communication open between me and those around me. I don't allow anger and disagreement to fester, and I encourage those around me to work out their differences without hurting one another.

• I know what I am living for. I am willing to "take the heat" and stand alone for what is right. I can take criticism without feeling self-pity or self-righteousness.

—LYMAN COLEMAN

BIBLE STUDY

1. Read the following passages. What is your response to each one?

| Micah 6:8 | Isaiah 58:6-9 |
| Matthew 25:31-40 | 1 John 2:3-6 |

2. What promises of God do we have for the hard times in our lives?

| John 16:33 | Romans 8:35-39 |
| 2 Corinthians 4:8-10 | |

3. Read Galatians 5:22-23. What qualities does God want to create in us?

4. What clues about the Christian life do you get from these Bible words?

Matthew 22:37-40	Colossians 3:12-17
Ephesians 4:1-3	Romans 7:21-25
Romans 8:1-2	

If you want to learn more about the Christian lifestyle, consider reading Jesus' Sermon on the Mount in Matthew 5–7, or Paul's great description of love in 1 Corinthians 13.

Questions for Discussion

1. Think of one Christian that you know and admire. In what ways would you wish to be like that person?

2. If Jesus is a model of what it means to be truly human, what clues do you get from his life about the kind of life God wants us to live?

3. Read Lyman Coleman's outline of what makes for a happy or blessed Christian life. (They are a paraphrase of Jesus' words in Matthew 5.) To what extent are those values a part of your daily life?

4. If your goal is "to participate in Christ's ministry and mission in the world," what actions might you take?

5. To what extent should Christians be a counterculture? In what ways is it all right to live in conformity with our society? In what areas is it wrong?

CHAPTER 6

How Do I Grow as a Christian?

WHEN GOD CALLS YOU TO BE A CHRISTIAN, YOU BECOME A Christian by grace, as a free gift. Christian development begins once you accept the gift of salvation and the new relationship that Christ offers. Maybe you were a Christian as a child, but drifted away, and now you're back to take another look as an adult and recommit yourself to Christ and the Christian way. So you embark on the Christian life. Welcome back!

Is the Christian life hard? No, it's not hard—it's impossible. Most of what you're asked to do is not natural—not to human beings as we are now. But you're not alone in this. Jesus puts his spirit within you and makes it possible for you to live his kind of life.

You can't do it all immediately, but you will learn. Begin where you are. Make honest attempts day by day, living out the meaning of your baptism. And as you make healing Godward choices, you will be transformed. I like the old prayer used in the musical *Godspell:* "Day by day, O dear Lord, three things I pray: To see thee more clearly, to love thee more dearly, to follow thee more nearly—day by day."

To energize this day-by-day transformation in you, God gives you gifts. In this chapter we'll open a few of these gifts: God's word, Holy Communion, prayer, and sharing the faith with others.

THE GIFT OF THE WORD

When the Book-of-the-Month Club asked its members to name the book that most influenced their lives, the Bible was the book that topped the list. For Christians, the Bible is more than a good book, it is the word of God. Through hearing it read, reading it, studying it, learning it by heart, and meditating on it, we grow as Christians.

If you were to have a face-to-face conversation with God, what would it be like? What would you ask God? What do you think God would say to you? Fortunately for us, God found a way to convey his character, detail his actions, record people's response, and communicate his values, attitudes, purposes, and plans. Reading the Bible is like going on-line with God. It is meant to be interactive. It's God's Web site for instruction, information, and inspiration, to help us develop a life worth living. Even more important, the Bible nourishes a living relationship with God. The Bible is not just for our information, but for our formation.

In one sense, the Bible is not a book, but a collection of books—sixty-six of them—written more than a thousand years ago by more than forty authors. Christians believe that God guided the process whereby these people wrote and the way in which these books were gathered into what we now call the Bible. God used these human writers and their writings the way he uses the water of Holy Baptism and the bread and wine of Holy Communion as a way to reach us. Through these writings, more than anything else, God wants us to get to know him in Jesus. The Bible is God's word, not because it is a holy rule book, but because it brings Jesus to us.

Is this Bible a reliable book? People have tried to prove, and disprove for that matter, that the Bible is the word of God. These arguments probably won't be as much help to you as your own experience reading it and trying to live by it. Recently two people shared their experiences of hearing the word of God through the Bible with me.

Brenda's life was breaking down. She searched every day for a way or place to "get fixed." Through all her searching, she said that she would cry every time she heard or read something from the Bible. She had no idea why. All she knew was that the Bible had greatly impacted her. As she continued to search for what was missing in her life, she found herself in our church. She said, "When you started reading from the Bible, all I could do was cry. It wasn't a cry of pain. It was a cry of relief. I knew in the Bible I could find what I was look-ing for. Today the Bible has become my most helpful companion in my life as a wife, mother, and friend."

I once taught in a beautiful old castle in Craheim, Germany. The owner of the castle was a tenderhearted baroness named Elizabeth, whose face radiated happiness. Elizabeth told me that as she and her husband were traveling years ago, they saw a calendar with these words from the Bible written on it: "As for me and my household, we will serve the Lord" (Joshua 24:15). They agreed that this was what they wanted to do with their lives. They dedicated their castle and the rest of their lives to serving God. Their "chance" encounter with those words from the Bible changed everything for them.

Your experience with the Bible may not be that dramatic, but it can be just as real and transforming. How can you begin to open yourself up to the Bible? Here are a few tips.

Step 1: Choose Your Bible.
The Bible was originally written mainly in Hebrew and Greek. It has been translated into English many times, so there are many translations of Bibles to choose from. Which should you choose?

There are some considerations to help you choose a Bible. If your church uses a particular translation in the worship services or classes, you may want that same translation for your personal use. You may want to ask your pastor to recommend a translation he or she considers both accurate and readable. The owner of a Christian bookstore near you may be able to show you Bibles with notes, study guides, questions for discussion, or plans for daily reading. A friend or Bible teacher may also have some good suggestions. The positive reality is that no matter how long you've been a Christian, no matter what your background, there is a Bible to met your needs.

Step 2: Read the Bible.

Reading the Bible feeds our souls and shapes our thoughts and actions. Daily reading produces tremendous results. But where do you start? Unlike most books, the best way to begin isn't necessarily to start at the beginning and read it straight through. But a strictly haphazard reading isn't a good idea either. What works best is some plan of regular systematic reading.

For someone with little experience in Bible reading, a great way to begin is to choose one of the four stories of Jesus' life, the Gospels. There are also "One Year" Bibles that include a guide for reading through the Bible in just one year. There are also devotional magazines, such as *Christ in Our Home* or *The Upper Room,* that will give you brief readings from the Bible with some explanatory comment.

Step 3: Study the Bible.

While you can gain much from simply reading the Bible, you will find more treasures if you study it. You can do this alone, using study guides and reference tools, but you may find even more value in studying with a group. Most churches offer a variety of Bible courses in group settings. A group gives you the advantage of an inspiring teacher, as well as someone with whom you can share your questions and discoveries.

Some people also find that memorizing key passages of the Bible helps them make these words their own. Mark the passages that especially speak to you, and commit them to memory. They are then available to you to meditate on and to work in your heart.

Step 4: Apply the Bible.

Bible reading or study is not just an intellectual exercise to fill our heads with more knowledge. Its deepest value is as part of an ongoing, active relationship with God.

Putting the Bible into practice in your life lays a solid foundation for building the best life possible. Applying what you read and study in the Bible plugs you into purpose, prescription, and power for living.

The way to know, understand, and experience God and all that he has for your life, is to become involved with God through his word. The Bible is more than words on paper. It changes lives. It can change yours. Reading the Bible won't always be exciting. The results won't always be evident in your life. But you can trust that God's spirit is working in you as you read, study, learn, and live with God's word.

THE GIFT OF THE HOLY MEAL

Only hours before his death, Jesus celebrated a sacred meal with his first followers. It is called the Lord's Supper, because it was Jesus himself who celebrated it first and told his followers to celebrate it forever. It is called Holy Communion because it is our communion, our relationship, with Jesus and with one another. Some Christians refer to it as the Eucharist. Roman Catholics may use the word Mass. Christians differ in what they call this holy meal, and in some details of the way they celebrate it. But all agree on some basic points.

Jesus said that we should eat the bread and wine together as a way of remembering him. We come to celebrate the Last Supper as a way of reminding ourselves who Jesus is and that we belong to him.

All Christians believe that through this Holy Communion we receive the forgiveness of sins. Along with the eating and drinking we receive God's promise of forgiveness. That forgiveness brings us new life and strengthens our relationship with God.

When Jesus celebrated the first Holy Communion, he said about the bread, "Take and eat. This is my body." About the wine, he said, "Drink from it. . . . This is my blood" (Matthew 26:26-28). Christians have argued a lot through the centuries about just what this means. Fortunately, you don't have to understand it. It's enough to believe that when you receive the bread and wine, Jesus is there with you, and you are with him.

THE GIFT OF PRAYER

Prayer is an expression of faith. People pray while sitting, kneeling, standing, walking, driving, or working. Nearly fifty percent of the world's population prays daily. Prayer puts us in touch and keeps us in touch with God.

When you pray, you don't need to use any special religious language. Talking to God as we talk with a friend is not only okay, it's important. It isn't necessary to convince God about what we need. Rather prayer is God's way of communicating with us about what God is eager, ready, and willing to do for us. God does answer every prayer. Sometimes the answer is yes, sometimes no, and sometimes wait.

Prayer is much more than a way to get things we need. It is a primary way we develop a relationship with God. We all know how important good communication is in any human relationship. It's equally important in our relationships with God and Jesus Christ.

If you want more ideas on how to pray, you may want to read my book *The Everyday, Anytime Guide to Prayer* (Augsburg Books). But ultimately, you will learn to pray best by praying.

THE GIFT OF FAITH SHARING

Receive the gift of faith and keep on growing in faith by finding and being with people who have it. We grow as Christians by being with other Christians. And that means being part of the church. Whether you're in a church or not, being with people of faith is the important thing.

We grow, then, as we talk together, worship together, share the Lord's Supper, and just be together. A lot happens when we share our faith stories—when I tell you my experience with God and you tell me yours. I can learn from your victories and your failures, and you can learn from mine.

This is what is usually meant by the term witnessing. You witness what you experience. To some people, witnessing sounds scary, and it can be sometimes. But remember what a witness in court needs to do. All she has to do is tell what she saw and heard. She only has to tell what she knows, no more, no less.

How do we best share our faith stories with other believers and seekers of Christian faith? I've developed a list I call "The Witnessing Top Ten":

1. Be transparent.

Transparency gives credibility to Christianity. Let others see your hurts, fears, questions, doubts, as well as your happiness, delights, and dreams. Anything that seems like confusing, insincere hype is quickly rejected. Claiming to be perfect, super-spiritual, or better than others diminishes the message as well as the messenger. Heart stuff is the good stuff. Let others see you as you really are—warts and all.

2. Be honest.

It is important to be honest about your challenges, disappointments, and struggles as a Christian—just as it is essential to be honest about supernatural experiences, victories, and amazing discoveries.

3. Be brief.

You might be tempted to share everything you know with people. It is better to be brief. And remember that actions, though brief, can be better than words. Words can often be confusing, but actions are always clear.

4. Be sensitive.

Being sensitive is sensible. Many people are afraid of Christians and churches. They may have had a bad experience in the past and need tender compassion more than religious talk. Others may need food, clothes, medicine, or housing before they are ready to listen or talk. A balance between sensitive observation and sensitive talking is the secret.

5. Be a good listener.

It is in understanding that we can be understood. To understand, it is essential to listen more than we talk. We need to listen with our hearts as well as our ears. The right to be heard is won by being a good listener.

6. Be gracious.

Grace—unqualified acceptance—is more powerful than criticism or judgment because this is what God showed us and what we are to show one another. My mother taught me that flies are caught with honey rather than with vinegar. Being gracious is the most appropriate expression of God's accepting, healing, and transforming power.

7. Be kind.

Harshness is offensive. Acts of kindness and gentleness make Christianity more irresistible. Christian bullies build barriers, not bridges, to faith. When you are kind, you let people know they are respected and valued. Our words and deeds can either heal or pierce the human heart. The greatest witness is a kind witness.

8. Be informed.

This means learning more about the Christian faith through group study, worship, and reading. Also getting to know Christ personally and intimately through prayer is essential to effective witnessing. Talking about a stranger is very different from talking about a friend. It is more convincing to share from personal experience than from second-hand information.

9. Be creative.

The creative witness is a motivating witness. Old religious clichés and tired metaphors are more easily dismissed than new and fresh ways of speaking. Tailoring our witness to the uniqueness of each individual produces tremendous results. Courageous creative conversation makes Christianity seem more inviting and exciting.

10. Be positive.

Christianity is about "good news"—the meaning of gospel or "good spell." It is news of hope, peace, and joy—and the love of God that never ends.

Guided by these ten principles you can share your faith confidently with fellow seekers—inside or outside the church. Then leave the results up to God. You are not responsible for your friend's reaction or response. You are not even ultimately responsible for your own growth. God will provide the growth—both to you and to your neighbor.

There's a lot in the Bible I just don't understand or can't believe. Do I have to accept it all in order to be a Christian?

Christianity is not about how much we believe in and understand God or the Bible. It's about how much God believes in and understands you and me. The Christian faith is not measured by how much we love God but by how much God loves us. A helpful guide would be: Accept as much as you can right now, and live according to the truth you can accept. God will take care of the rest.

How can the bread and wine of Communion really be the body and blood of Jesus?

This is a mystery. We do not understand how Jesus gives us his body and blood through Holy Communion, but he promised he would. For me, that settles it. It's not true because I believe it. It's true because Jesus said it.

What kind of people will help me grow as a Christian?

Finding people we can relate to readily is a good place to begin. For me, one of the most important considerations is Christian character. People who behave as they believe have integrity and are good coaches and mentors.

One idea I've found helpful: We need people who are ahead of us on the Christian road, some who are at the about the same place we are, and some behind us who we can help along the way.

You can pray that God will bring these kinds of people into your life—exactly the ones you need. Keep in mind that some of the people who can help you grow may not be people you meet face-to-face, but through books.

I've been a Christian for a while, but I don't feel that I'm growing? Is there something wrong?

Growth is a lifelong process. Many areas of life need to be put on the growing edge: our attitudes, actions, language, relationships, habits, lifestyle, and our use of time. At the end of each year, I look back to the beginning and honestly evaluate where I've grown and where I haven't. I set growth goals for myself and write them down so I can evaluate them later.

Keep in mind that we can't always see our own growth. This is one area where a spiritual mentor or friend can help us.

THOUGHTS FOR REFLECTION

This life is not a being holy, but a becoming holy; it is not a being well, but a getting well; it is not a being, but a becoming. It is not inactivity but practice. . . . As yet we are not what we ought to be, but we are getting there; the task is not yet accomplished and completed, but it is in progress and pursuit. The end has not yet been reached, but we are on the way that leads to it.

—MARTIN LUTHER

When we worship and celebrate joyfully, we release powerful healing forces within ourselves. When a person consciously sets aside burdens or pain in order to celebrate, he or she is saying, in effect, that God's life is far more important than any problems they are struggling with. . . . Through celebration, the Christian can participate more fully in the resurrection of Christ, who is the dance at the heart of all things.

—MARILYN HOOD

A shift in my own understanding of the Bible came when I realized that things are not true because they are in the Bible. Rather, things are in the Bible because they are true.

—KEITH MILLER AND BRUCE LARSON

The only way to pray is to pray; and the way to pray well is to pray much. If one has not time for this, then one must at least pray regularly. But the less one prays, the worse it goes.

—DOM JOHN CHAPMAN

Bible Study

1. What do each of these Bible passages teach us about the goals of Christian growth? How would you summarize these teachings? Growing as a Christian means . . .

Ephesians 4:14-16   Ephesians 4:22-24
Colossians 2:6-7   John 15:4-5

2. Read Philippians 3:12-14. Which words suggest effort or struggle in the Christian life?

3. What does the Bible teach about itself in these passages?

2 Timothy 3:14-17   John 20:30-31
James 1:22-25   Matthew 7:24-25

QUESTIONS FOR DISCUSSION

1. What has been your experience with the Bible?

2. What are your attitudes and thoughts about the Lord's Supper?

3. To what extent is prayer a part of your life?

4. How would you most like to grow as a Christian?

5. What do you think you need most to grow personally as a Christian?

CHAPTER 7

Is There Hope for the Future?

ONE DAY I TOOK A VIDEO CREW TO ARROWHEAD SHOPPING Mall, just down the road from our church, to videotape responses to the question, "How do you get to heaven?" Here are some of the answers:

"By being a good person."

"Right through the front door."

"My baby brother died, and he got to go to heaven."

"By being kind to animals."

"By not breaking the Ten Commandments."

"Why would I want to go to heaven? All my friends are down there!"

Can all of these people be right? Are any of them right? Is "How do you get to heaven?" really the right question? Starting with a more basic question about heaven will help clear up the confusion about how we get there.

WHERE GOD IS, THERE IS HEAVEN

What is heaven like? Through the centuries people have thought of heaven as "up there" somewhere above the clouds. We've sent astronauts, unmanned vehicles and space telescopes beyond the earth to probe the depths of the galaxies and we haven't seen heaven. Does that mean heaven does not exist? No, heaven is a reality, but not that kind of reality.

Heaven is God's home, and where God is, there is heaven. Where the king is, there is the kingdom. When you become a Christian, God's own spirit lives with you, and heaven becomes a part of your life here and now. Heaven begins with a radiant relationship with Jesus Christ. Heaven isn't simply a destination, it is a continuous journey with God.

Life is not to be divided with a life today on earth and life tomorrow in heaven. We are already citizens of eternity. By acting and thinking like citizens of heaven, we can begin to experience everlasting life in this life.

I have felt God's presence in this world. I have seen God's hand at work in my own life, bringing people and circumstances together in a way I never could have engineered or imagined. When I see God's hand at work, I know that heaven is here right now, an intrinsic part of the world God created. Knowing Jesus opens my spirit and my understanding to see and participate in heaven in my daily life; knowing Jesus makes the ordinary extraordinary.

Having a heavenly perspective now is like standing on the rim of the Grand Canyon. Rafting the Colorado River in the steep inner gorge of the canyon, you often can't see what is around the next bend, much less where the river is going. But from a vantage point above on the rim, you can see glimpses of the river's course. Flying over the canyon at 30,000 feet, you can easily follow the river as it flows from north to south.

When we're on the river of daily life, with the rush of rapids ahead and the walls of circumstances closing in on us, it's hard to see where the river is taking us. But having a heavenly perspective now, like standing on the rim, lifts me up to see something of God's direction and purpose in my life. This gives me courage, faith, and the power to steer my thoughts and actions. I can run the river effectively, wisely and joyfully now, knowing that one day I'll fly above and see the whole course of my life with new understanding.

Recognizing that we are already experiencing eternal life with God here on earth, empowers us to truly live each day, so that our epitaph won't read: Here Lies John Doe, died at 35, buried at 85.

So heaven is a quality of life of being with God that begins already here on earth. But this life ends in death for all of us. For each one of us—and for our friends and loved ones—death brings an end to this kind of life. What then?

The answer is found in a promise Jesus made to his first followers and to us: "Do not let your hearts be troubled. Trust in God; trust also in me. In my Father's house are many rooms; if it were not so, I would have told you. I am going there to prepare a place for you" (John 14:1). Jesus himself is preparing a place for you and me. When we try to describe this place, we are limited by our understanding. We are forced into the kind of language that we use for the most true of truths—the language of poetry, of imagery of streets of gold. No one, not even those people who have had near-death experiences, can tell about it. So where do we begin to look for something more concrete, for reliable information about heaven? The logical place to start is with God.

Whatever and wherever heaven may be, there are several things of which you can be sure: at this very moment, Jesus is in heaven praying for you and preparing a place for you. Heaven is a place of unfathomable love. And heaven is the future home of believers. Joni Earackson Tada writes:

> Heaven is your journey's end, your life's goal, your purpose for going on. If heaven is the home of your spirit, the rest for your soul, the repository of every spiritual investment on earth, then it must grip your heart. And your heart must grip heaven by faith.

What makes the promise of heaven so exciting is not what we'll see, but whom we'll see: the God who loves us. The most important thing is that we will be with God in a more complete way than we can be now on earth.

But what we will be in heaven also is exciting. The Bible promises that in heaven Jesus will "transform our lowly bodies so that they will be like his glorious body." We will not cease to be human beings in heaven. We will not be disembodied spirits or angels. But the bodies we will have will be transformed into something we can only dream of now.

Heaven will be a time of divine fulfillment. We will not stop growing in heaven. All that limits us here will be removed. Our potential will be fully realized. We will become all that God destined for us to be. Heaven is our earthly journey's end and the beginning of an adventure we can't even begin to conceive.

What is the way to this place Jesus has prepared for us? There is only one way. The highway to heaven is by God's grace through faith in Jesus Christ. The message of the Christian faith is that trusting Jesus Christ with our lives provides everything we need to get to heaven.

Doorway to God

For a Christian, death is the doorway that opens to reveal the face of our loving God. At the age of six, Kelly had undergone surgery to remove a malignant brain tumor. Then began months of radiation, chemotherapy, and blood transfusions. Kelly had told her mother, "I'm not afraid of dying, because I know I'll be with Jesus. I'm just afraid of how I might die."

One morning Kelly came into the kitchen and said to her mother, "I had the best dream, I dreamed I was with Jesus." Her mother asked, "How did you know it was Jesus?" Kelly responded, "I just knew. We were eating together and the table was wrapped in light."

A few weeks later, Kelly died. Cleaning her room, her mother found a notebook in which she had written shortly after her dream:

> Dear Jesus, I really felt much closer to you these past years, and I still do. I have felt your presence more. I thank you for this time of cancer through the past year and a half. It has given me a time to get even closer to you. I am so excited to come to your kingdom some day. I don't know anything about what heaven will be like, but I know it's going to be the best place I have ever been. It feels so good to know that I'm in your arms, safe and sound!

At the memorial service for Kelly, her parents received a note in a childish scrawl: "Dear Kelly, enjoy your supper with God."

When Jesus wanted to explain what faith is like, he pointed to the trust of little children. I can see why.

Jesus has gone to prepare a place for us. We were born for such a place. That's the hope and promise of heaven, and we can begin to experience it right now.

We know that our future lies secure with God, that we will spend eternity in the presence of the loving God as totally transformed persons. Jesus has promised even more than that. He promised that he is coming again, that he will return at the end of time to bring God's dream for the whole universe to completion. God will not give up on his creation, but will see his plans fulfilled. Here our imaginations falter, but the Bible promises that there will be "a new heaven and a new earth" (Revelation 21:1). Just as we will be transformed on the other side of death to become truly our best selves, so God will transform all his creation to fulfill his highest dreams.

That is the hope that God gives us. That is the hope that brightens our lives—now and eternally.

My grandmother died last week. Where is she now?

Your grandmother is with God. The Bible promises that for all God's people there will never be a moment, dead or alive, that we will be without God. When our eyes close for the last time one earth, the next thing we will see is the loving face of God. Jesus said to one of the thieves crucified with him, "Today you will be with me in paradise" (Luke 23:43). Your grandmother is safely in the hands of a loving God.

I want to believe in heaven, but why does there have to be a hell? Would God really condemn people in hell forever?

Hell is living separated from God. Those who have chosen to reject God's invitation to follow him will experience the consequences of their choice. God desires everyone to be saved, but no one is forced to live all and only for Christ. God has given us the freedom to choose against him. God also honors the use of freedom that leads to eternal life.

The Bible speaks of a day of judgment. This judgment will not introduce anything new into our lives. It will simply reveal what our life has been like all along. Christians do not have to fear the judgment of God because we place our trust in Jesus our Savior.

Instead of dreaming about heaven, shouldn't we concentrate on making life on this planet better?
If we are not settled with heaven, we remain unsettled on earth. People who are not ready to die are not ready to live. Once the eternal destiny issue is taken care of, we are free to lay our life on the line for the greatest adventure imaginable.

THOUGHTS FOR REFLECTION

A man or woman without hope in the future cannot live creatively in the present. The paradox of expectation is that those who believe in tomorrow can better live today, that those who expect joy to come from sadness can discover the beginnings of new life in the center of the old, that those who look forward to the returning Lord can discover him already in their midst.

—HENRI NOUWEN

We will not lose in heaven. We will gain. . . . Somehow, somewhere within you is the pattern of the heavenly person you will become, and if you want to catch a glimpse of how glorious and full of splendor your body will be, just do a comparison. Compare a hairy peach pit with the tree it becomes, loaded with fragrant blossoms and sweet fruit.

—JONI EARACKSON TADA

The remark so often made that "Heaven is a state of mind" bears witness to the wintry and deathlike phase of the process in which we are now living. The implication is that if heaven is a state of mind—or, more correctly, of the spirit—then it must be only a state of the spirit. . . . That is what every great religion except Christianity would say. . . . by teaching the resurrection of the body it teaches that Heaven is not merely a state of the sprit but a state of the body as well; and therefore a state of Nature as a whole.

—C. S. LEWIS

It is an offense to God to give up hope and to live as if our history is but one catastrophe after another building up to one final, colossal holocaust. Anticipation of Christ's return and a "new Jerusalem" comes not from weariness with struggling against the evil forces in this world. It comes from the promise that this world at its very best is but a glimpse of something infinitely more fulfilling to come. Longing for God's heaven comes not from a repudiation of God's earth, but from hunger for the goodness and beauty that we have tasted here.

—ALVIN N. ROGNESS

BIBLE STUDY

1. What does the Bible say about hope?
   Romans 8:18-25   Romans 15:13
   1 Timothy 6:17-19

2. What does the Bible say about heaven?
   John 14:1-3   Acts 7:54-56
   Philippians 3:20-21   2 Peter 3:13

3. What does the Bible say about the way to heaven?
   John 17:3   John 3:16
   1 Peter 1:3-5   John 6:40

QUESTIONS FOR DISCUSSION

1. What are your thoughts and feelings as you think about the future?

2. What gives you most hope for your own life and for the life of humankind?

3. How would you answer the question: How do you get to heaven?

4. As you think back over your study of this book, what did you find most helpful?

5. What questions about the Christian faith do you still have? Where can you look for answers?

Acknowledgments

The author gratefully acknowledges the following sources for their contributions to this book. Any omissions are unintentional and will be corrected upon future printings.

CHAPTER 1: HOW CAN I KNOW ABOUT GOD?

Edwin Carlson, quoted in *Don Bierle, Surprised by Faith,* Lynwood, Wash.: Emerald Books, 1992: 81.

Paul Davies, *The Mind of God: The Scientific Basis for a Rational World,* New York: Simon & Schuster, Touchstone Books, 1993: 16.

Thomas Kelly, *Testament of Devotion,* New York: Harper & Bros., 1941: 18–19.

A. W. Tozer, *The Pursuit of God,* Harrisburg, Penn.: Christian Publications, 1948: 107.

J. I. Packer, *Knowing God,* Downers Grove, Ill.: InterVarsity Press, 1973: 29.

C. S. Lewis, *Mere Christianity,* New York: Macmillan, 1943: 142–43. Used by permission of HarperCollins Publishers UK.

CHAPTER 2: WHO IS THIS JESUS?

Keith Miller, *A Taste of New Wine,* Waco, Texas: Word, 1969: 31–32.

Dorothy Sayers, *The Whimsical Christian,* New York: Macmillan, 1978: 14.

C. S. Lewis, *Mere Christianity,* 54–55.

Peter Marshall, *The Best of Peter Marshall,* Old Tappan, N.J.: Chosen Books, 1983: 57.

CHAPTER 3: WHY BOTHER ABOUT SIN?

Robert L. Short, *The Parables of Peanuts,* New York: Harper & Row, 1968: 49.

Max Lucado, *In the Grip of Grace*, Dallas: Word, 1996: 62.

C. S. Lewis, *Mere Christianity:* 58–59.

C. S. Lewis, ed., *George Macdonald, An Anthology,* London: Geoffrey Bles: The Centenary Press, 1946: 87.

Alvin N. Rogness, *The Book of Comfort,* Minneapolis: Augsburg Books, 1979: 28.

CHAPTER 4: HOW DO I BECOME A CHRISTIAN?

Jimmy Carter, *Living Faith,* New York: Random House, 1996: 20.

Henri Nouwen, *Letters to Marc About Jesus,* New York: Harper & Row, 1987: 61.

Rachel Hosmer and Alan Jones, *Living in the Spirit,* New York: Seabury, 1979: 132–33.

H. George Anderson, *A Good Time to Be the Church,* Minneapolis: Augsburg Books, 1997: 30.

Alvin N. Rogness, *The Book of Comfort,* 88–89.

Chapter 5: How Do I Live the Christian Life?

Billy Graham, *Just as I Am,* San Francisco: HarperCollins, 1997: 722.

Douglas John Hall, *Why Christian?* Minneapolis: Fortress Press, 1998: 86.

Alan Sager, *Gospel-Centered Spirituality,* Minneapolis: Augsburg Books, 1990: 78–79.

Rich Bimler in Cal and Rose Samra, *Holy Humor,* Nashville: Thomas Nelson, 1997: 238.

Michael Warren, "Catechesis and Spirituality" in *Religious Education,* Vol. 83, No. 1.

Lyman Coleman in *The NIV Serendipity Bible for Study Groups,* © Serendipity House, Grand Rapids: Zondervan, 1988: 1245.

Chapter 6: How Do I Grow as a Christian?

Martin Luther, *What Luther Says, Vol. 1,* Ewald Plass, ed. St.Louis: Concordia, 1987: 235.

Marilyn Hood in Cal and Rose Samra, *Holy Humor,* 238.

Keith Miller and Bruce Larson, *The Edge of Adventure,* Waco, Texas: Word, 1975: 71–72.

Dom Chapman, *The Spiritual Letters of Dom Chapman,* Kansas City, Mo.: Sheed and Ward, 1935: 53.

Chapter 7: Is There Hope for the Future?

Joni Earackson Tada, *Heaven: Your Real Home,* Grand Rapids: Zondervan, 1995: 23.

Henri J. M. Nouwen, *Out of Solitude*, Notre Dame, Ind.: Ave Maria Press, 1974: 59.

Joni Earackson Tada, *Heaven: Your Real Home:* 28, 38.

C. S. Lewis, *Miracles,* New York: Macmillan, 1947: 67. Used by permission of HarperCollins Publishers UK.

Alvin N. Rogness, *The Book of Comfort:* 138.

Books to Grow On

Holmes, Marjorie. *Two from Galilee.* Old Tappan, N.J.: F. H. Revell Co., 1986.

Hybels, Bill and Mark Mittelberg. *Becoming a Contagious Christian.* Grand Rapids, Mich.: Zondervan Publishing House, 1994.

Lucado, Max. *God Came Near: Chronicles of the Christ.* Portland, Oreg.: Multnomah Press, 1987.

McDowell, Josh. *More Than a Carpenter.* Wheaton, Ill.: Tyndale House Pub., 1977.

Sheldon, Charles M. *In His Steps.* Grand Rapids, Mich.: Chosen Books, 1984.

Strobel, Lee. *God's Outrageous Claims: Thirteen Discoveries That Can Revolutionize Your Life.* Grand Rapids, Mich.: Zondervan Publishing House, 1997.

Sweet, Leonard. *The Jesus Prescription for a Healthy Life.* Nashville, Tenn.: Abingdon Press, 1996.

Swindoll, Charles R. *Simple Faith.* Dallas, Tex.: Word Pub., 1991.

Verploegh, Harry. *The Oswald Chambers Devotional Reader: 52 Weekly Themes.* Nashville, Tenn.: Oliver Nelson, 1990.

Yancey, Philip. *The Jesus I Never Knew.* Grand Rapids, Mich.: Zondervan Publishing House, 1995.